better together*

*This book is best read together, grownup and kid.

a kids
book
about

a kids book about

PUBLIC HEALTH

by Becca Yanniello

a
kids
book
about

Printed in the United States of America.

A Kids Book About books are available online: *akidsco.com*

To share your stories, ask questions, or inquire about bulk
purchases (schools, libraries, and nonprofits), please use
the following email address: *hello@akidsco.com*

Print ISBN: 978-1-958825-43-3
Ebook ISBN: 978-1-958825-44-0

Designed by Rick DeLucco
Edited by Emma Wolf

For Connor and Siena.

May you always dream big
and lead with love.

Intro

When someone first told me about public health, I had to Google it! That's because when public health policies and services are doing their job, no one really notices—we just stay healthy!

It isn't until something goes wrong, like a contaminated water supply or a global pandemic, that public health is brought into the spotlight. Yet, it impacts our lives every day by removing threats to our health and keeping us safe.

The field of **public health** is like a big umbrella that covers a broad range of research, policies, services, education, and more. It impacts everything from our food and water, to vaccinations and sanitation. The common thread is the goal to give everyone the opportunity and resources to be healthy.

We all know that responsive medical care is important, but wouldn't it be great if we could avoid sickness and injuries in the first place? I hope by reading this book, you will gain a new appreciation for the things that are happening all around us to do just that.

What if I told you there was something that impacts all of us that you've probably never heard of?

What if it mattered for you, your family, friends, school, and everyone else on the planet, and it's always been right there in plain sight?

Hard to imagine, right?

Well, it's true!

And that thing, that

HUGE THING

that affects everyone, is...

PUBLIC

HEALTH!

You might think public health sounds kinda boring.

And if you've never heard of it before, you might think it doesn't make a difference in your life.

But I wrote this book to convince you and every other kid that it matters so much more than any of us could ever imagine.

SO, WHAT IS PUBLIC HEALTH?

Public health is a field of science that is all about protecting and promoting health.

That means *preventing* things that make us sick and unhealthy, like disease, pollution, and injuries.

It also means *protecting* things we need to stay healthy, like ensuring every community has access to doctors, clean water, clean air, and safe places to live, go to school, work, and play.

And the goal of public health
is to have the biggest impact
possible on the most people!

While doctors and nurses
treat 1 patient at a time,
public health workers
help groups of people.

Public health workers also focus on what's happening outside of hospitals and clinics—in places like our schools, homes, and communities—to help prevent people from getting sick or injured.

And, guess what?
When public health work is at play,
everyone wins! Seriously!

Public health makes life
better for you, your family,
your community, and the world.

DO YOU BELIEVE ME YET?

Well, let me give you some examples!

We have clean water to drink because public health creates rules to keep chemicals and waste out of our water supply.

We wear seatbelts because public health is about taking steps to prevent injuries and accidents.

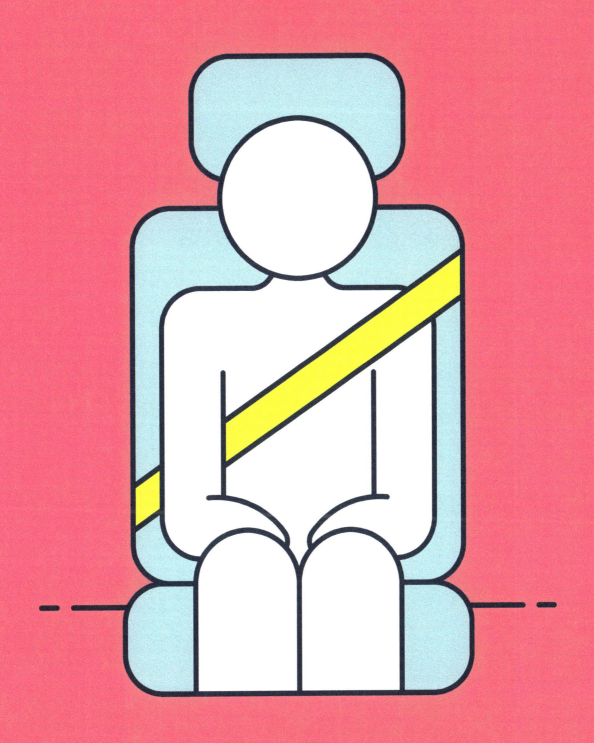

Foods we buy at the store and at restaurants are safe to eat because public health creates standards for how those foods are produced (so no one gets sick)!

And here are a ton of other things that exist because of the science of public health:

See what I mean
about public health
helping everyone?

Now, I want you to imagine that the science of public health didn't exist.

Like, say, people didn't wash their hands...ever!

Maybe you think that wouldn't be a big deal.

It's actually a **HUGE** deal and used to happen often.

Until the 1840s, people (even doctors!) didn't think washing their hands was important.

And guess what happened? A lot of people got really sick.

ALL. THE. TIME.

No one knew why until scientists discovered that little things called germs can get passed from person to person.

And if we don't wash our hands, they stick around and get us sick.

Public health research
and policies changed all that.

Now, we wash our hands because
we know we can keep ourselves
and others healthy by washing
away those germs instead of
spreading them around!

SO, HOW DOES PUBLIC HEALTH WORK?

Glad you asked!

Public health scientists study what is making people sick and what is keeping them healthy.

Then, based on what they discover, public health officials create policies and services that help everyone stay healthy and safe.

Public health for individuals looks like:

Education, which helps us
make healthy choices, and vaccines
that keep us and the people
around us healthy.

Public health for families looks like:

Having access to healthy food
and feeling safe in our homes
(remember, smoke detectors!).

Public health for communities looks like:

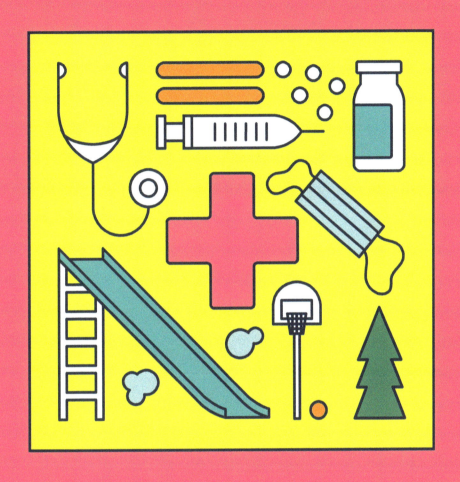

Having enough doctors who understand the language and culture of the people they are helping, and having safe parks and playgrounds for everyone.

Public health for cities looks like:

Healthy foods for school lunches and reliable trash removal for our waste.

Public health for countries looks like:

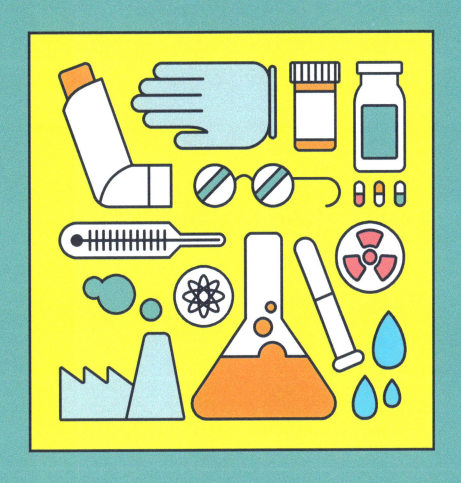

Having policies that keep unsafe chemicals out of the water and air, and ensuring there are enough medications and vaccines for everyone who needs them.

Public health for the world looks like:

Responding to natural disasters by providing food, water, and shelter.

Look how much you just
learned about public health!

Now that you know all of this,
I want you to try something...

LOOK AROUND.

That's right! I want you to look around and notice where public health makes a difference in your life.

LOOK
in your home.

LOOK
at your local park.

LOOK
around your school.

I want you to notice what is in place to keep you and your community healthy and safe.

How many things can you find?

What impact do you think they have?

Now go 1 step further.

I want you to think about
what could be even better.

What in your world could change to make you and your community even more healthy?

Public health is all about creating a healthier world for everyone.

And remember, even a simple idea, like washing your hands...

CAN CHANGE THE WORLD FOR THE BETTER!

Outro

My favorite part about working in public health is the positive impact it has for people everywhere. Advances in public health help people live longer, healthier lives than just a few generations ago. Pretty amazing!

But, even with these advances, health disparities exist everywhere in the world. Did you know that where you live can impact your health just as much (or more!) as your genes? An important role of public health is to research these disparities, understand them, find their cause, and address them head on.

So, how do we talk about this with kids? Start by asking:

Why is it important for everyone to have an equal chance to be healthy?

What do you think it takes to be healthy and feel our best?

How can we make that possible for everyone?

Public health is about improving the health of our communities, our world, and generations to come. So let's roll up our sleeves. We have work to do!

About The Author

Becca (she/her) is a public health professional devoted to improving the health of populations, big and small. She holds a master's in public health from UCLA and a bachelor of arts in psychology from the University of Southern California. She has worked for government, nonprofit, and large healthcare organizations, developing and overseeing health programs and services for people across southern California. Her belief that everyone should have the resources and opportunity to be healthy drives her to focus on serving vulnerable and underserved populations.

Becca was born and raised in the Pacific Northwest, but discovered year-round sunshine and has lived in Los Angeles ever since. She is an avid traveler and lifelong learner. But most importantly, she is a mother of 2 beautiful kids, who remind her that anything is possible.

in @becca-yanniello-4627925

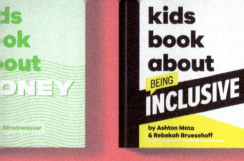
kids book about ...ONEY
...by Stramwasser

kids book about **BEING INCLUSIVE**
by Ashton Mota & Rebekah Bruesehoff

kids book about diversity
by Charnaie Gordon

kids book about **LEADER SHIP**
by Orion Jean

ki bo ab IMM
by MJ C

a kids book about **SAFETY**
by Soraya Sutherlin, CEM
in partnership with JUDY

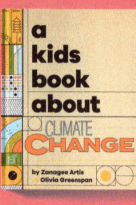
a kids book about **CLIMATE CHANGE**
by Zanagee Artis & Olivia Greenspan

a kids book about **IMAGINATION**
by LEVAR BURTON

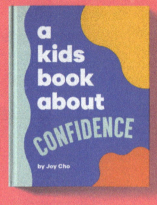
a kids book about **CONFIDENCE**
by Joy Cho

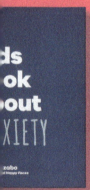
kids ok out ...XIETY
...zabo
Happy Faces

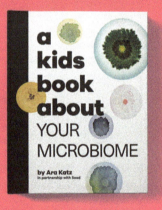
a kids book about **YOUR MICROBIOME**
by Ara Katz
in partnership with Seed

a kids book about **racism**
by Jelani Memory

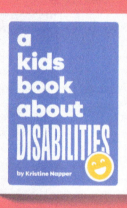
a kids book about **DISABILITIES**
by Kristine Napper

a ki b ak bo
by KYL

a kids book about ...VORCE
...Ashley Simpo

a kids book about **cancer**
by Dr. Kelsie Storm & Sarah Porter

a kids book about **BEING TRANSGENDER**
by Gia Parr
in partnership with The GenderCool Project

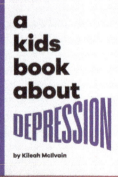
a kids book about **DEPRESSION**
by Kileah McIlvain

...ds ok out ...ame

a kids book about **THE TULSA**

Printed in the USA
CPSIA information can be obtained
at www.ICGtesting.com
LVHW071836110823
754949LV00015B/785